DOG
ALPHABET

Words by Robin Feiner

A is for American Pit Bull Terrier. This breed often gets a bad rap as being dangerous and aggressive. But the truth is, Pit Bulls are actually warm and gentle. They're also loyal, brave and smart, making them perfect service and therapy dogs.

B is for Beagle.
They're the clever hunting hounds with an expert sense of smell. Boasting just the right balance of assertiveness, friendliness and energy, Beagles are packed with personality and aren't afraid to express themselves.
Loud and proud!

C is for Border **C**ollie. Famous for being hard-working herders, agility superstars and prize-winning show dogs, Collies are equal parts athletic, obedient and smart. In fact, the most intelligent dog in the world happens to be a Border Collie named Chaser! Legend.

D is for **D**achshund. Described as a half-dog high and a dog-and-a-half long, these sausage dogs with warm, loving eyes are playful and fun. Using their keen sense of smell and stubborn determination, they are fearless when it comes to the chase!

E is for English Bulldog. Although this smooshy-faced breed is calm and friendly, it's also courageous and determined. That's why it's the mascot for the U.S. Marine Corps, as well as many sports teams across the United States, United Kingdom, Canada and Australia. Go, Bulldogs!

F is for French Bulldog. Frenchies are affectionate and super-sensitive with a whole range of emotions! They'll often talk to you using growls, howls, yawns and gargles, and mope around if they're upset. Never a dull moment with these amusing pups!

G is for **G**erman Shepherd.
Because they're so smart
and strong, these clever K-9s
make excellent police rescue
dogs and military soldiers.
They were even trained to
parachute out of airplanes
during the World Wars!
A big salute to these
legendary hard-workers.

H is for Alaskan **H**usky. With their thick double coat and fluffy body, these gorgeous canines are built for the snow. Whether they're pulling a sled or digging under fences, they enjoy having a job to do and just love being around people. Naww!

I is for Irish Wolfhound. From Ancient Romans to Persian shahs and American presidents, these wolfdogs of Ireland are admired the world over. And even though they stand at a magnificent 7 feet tall (on their hind legs), they're actually quirky, quiet and sweet.

J is for Jack Russell Terrier. Extremely athletic and fearless, Jack Russells are fox hunting dogs by nature, which is why they can go and go and go! With their endless energy and noisy bark, they're a small dog with a big attitude!

K is for Cavalier **K**ing Charles. This regal lapdog got its name from the laid-back King Charles II himself, who was the proud owner of these comforter spaniels. With their beautiful smooth coat and soft brown eyes, Cavies are charming in any color.

L is for Labrador Retriever. Just like the Golden Retriever, Labradors have a cheeky, fun-loving side that is curious about absolutely everything! Intelligent, athletic and eager to please, Labs are the most popular breed in Australia, Canada, New Zealand, the U.K. and the U.S.!

M is for Mastiff.
Holding the record for the world's heaviest breed at 343 pounds, Mastiffs are a giant among dogs! You wouldn't think that such a massive, powerful-looking pooch would be calm and gentle, but they are exactly that. Get ready for cuddles!

N is for **N**ewfoundland. Thanks to their thick coat and webbed paws, these Canadian working dogs are natural long-distance swimmers and expert water rescue dogs. Noble and sweet – and weighing up to 150 pounds – Newfies are ever the gentle giants.

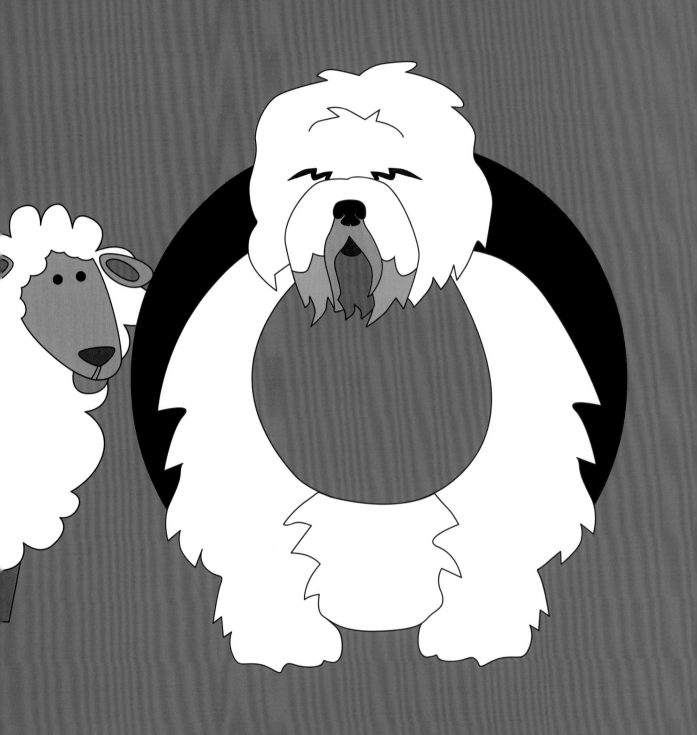

O is for **O**ld English Sheep Dog. With their shaggy coat covering their face and eyes, bear-like walk, and bark that sounds like two pots clanging together, Bobtails have a fun, clownish energy! They might even give you a nudge and try to herd you!

P is for **P**ug.
They're charming, cheerful and will do anything for a belly rub! First bred in Ancient China, Pugs were then later brought over to Europe, where even Queen Victoria and Marie Antoinette couldn't resist their cute, smooshy faces!

Q is for Queensland Heeler. Also known as the Australian Cattle Dog, these hard-working sheepdogs are popular with farmers and ranchers. That's because they can work from sunrise to sunset, herding livestock across wide open spaces. Aussie legends, getting the job done!

R is for Rottweiler. Because these majestic canines are naturally protective, they're often seen as aggressive. But lovers of the breed know that Rotties have a soft side that makes them excellent service, therapy and guide dogs, as well as loving family members.

S is for **S**aint Bernard.
They're big, they're powerful
and they drool – a lot!
Famously used in rescue
operations, they're also
patient and sociable, and
love being part of the family.

T is for Toy Poodle. Cuteness overload! This loveable little breed is the smallest of the Poodle family – and the proudest. They will wow you with their agility and obedience, and win you over with their elegance and warmth.

U is for **Ut**onagan.
Is that a dog or a wolf?!
Its name means 'spirit of
the wolf,' and that's exactly
what this breed was created
to look like, by crossing
five mixed-breed rescue
dogs with a Siberian Husky,
German Shepherd and
Alaskan Malamute.

V is for Vizsla.
The Hungarian hunting dog with a warm auburn coat and large droopy ears is certainly high-energy. Known for being extremely attached to their owners and sociable to strangers, Vizslas are the original Velcro dogs. They just want to stick to you!

W is for **W**elsh Corgi. They may be tiny with little legs and small tails, but they are fast runners with big personalities! They're also smart, cuddly and very sociable – and have been members of the British royal family for decades!

X is for **X**oloitzcuintli (sho-lo-its-queent-lee). This Mexican hairless breed believed to have mystic powers has been around for at least 3,500 years, making it the oldest breed known to humans. Historians have even found drawings of Xolos on ancient Aztec cave walls! Legendary.

Yy

Y is for Yorkshire Terrier. They may be the smallest ever doggo recorded in history, but judging by their boldness, you'd never know it! Brave and fiercely loyal, Yorkies certainly don't let their size hold them back from protecting their owners.

Z is for **Z**uchon.
A mix of Shih Tzu and Bichon Frise, these designer teddy bears also known as Shichons, love to be the center of attention! Playful and full of energy, they are eager to please their owners and everyone else they meet!

The ever-expanding legendary library

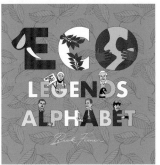

EXPLORE THESE LEGENDARY ALPHABETS & MORE AT WWW.ALPHABETLEGENDS.COM

DOG ALPHABET
www.alphabetlegends.com

Published by Alphabet Legends Pty Ltd in 2020
Created by Beck Feiner
Copyright © Alphabet Legends Pty Ltd 2020

UNICEF AUSTRALIA
A portion of the Net Proceeds from the sale of this book
are donated to UNICEF.

9780648962823